DOGS & DRAGONS

TREES & DREAMS

Books by Karla Kuskin

ABCDEFGHIJKLMNOPQRSTUVWXYZ
ALEXANDER SOAMES: HIS POEMS
ALL SIZES OF NOISES
THE ANIMALS AND THE ARK
ANY ME I WANT TO BE
THE BEAR WHO SAW THE SPRING
IN THE FLAKY, FROSTY MORNING
IN THE MIDDLE OF THE TREES
JAMES AND THE RAIN
JUST LIKE EVERYONE ELSE
NEAR THE WINDOW TREE
ROAR AND MORE
THE ROSE ON MY CAKE
SAND AND SNOW
A SPACE STORY
SQUARE AS A HOUSE
THE WALK THE MOUSE GIRLS TOOK
WATSON, THE SMARTEST DOG IN THE U.S.A.
WHAT DID YOU BRING ME?
WHICH HORSE IS WILLIAM?

HARPER & ROW, PUBLISHERS

NEW YORK

Cambridge
Hagerstown
Philadelphia
San Francisco

London
Mexico City
São Paulo
Sydney

1817

DOGS & DRAGONS
TREES & DREAMS

A Collection of Poems by

Karla Kuskin

Library of Congress Cataloging in Publication Data
Kuskin, Karla.
    Dogs and dragons, trees and dreams.

    SUMMARY: A representative collection of Karla Kuskin's
poetry with introductory notes on poetry writing and
appreciation.
    1. Children's poetry, American.   [1. American
poetry]   I. Title
PS3561.U79D6 1980   811'.54   79-2814
ISBN 0-06-023543-8
ISBN 0-06-023544-6 (lib. bdg.)

First Edition
    2   3   4   5   6   7   8   9   10

AN INTRODUCTION CHILDREN
MAY FEEL FREE TO IGNORE

The double purpose of this introduction is to bring together poems I wrote for children between 1958 and 1975 and to discuss the process of introducing poetry to children.

In addition to their common place of origin and span of time, these verses share basic elements of simple poetry: emphasis on rhythm, word sounds and, sometimes, rhyme and humor.

Rhyme isn't nearly as fashionable as it once was, but there's a lot of it here. Children enjoy reading it, reciting it and hearing it read. The swing and syllables of rhyming stick in the mind and stay on the tongue, often for a lifetime. Many of the enclosed are members of a happy family that includes song lyrics, jump rope jingles, tongue twisters and so on. One answer to "How do you introduce children to poetry?" is to begin with these relaxed, funny, rhythmical forms. Let the children you know get to feel at home with the family.

One introduction leads to another. The poetry reader often becomes a poetry writer. What could be better? No imagination is freer than a child's, no eye is sharper. The conversation of young children is a constant reminder that they are natural poets. But fitting unrestrained thoughts into rigid forms can be discouraging and may cramp the eccentric voice that makes a child's work (any work) unique. Read rhymes to children, but encourage them, as they begin to write, to write without rhyming. To write any way at all. And to read everything, anything . . . more poetry.

FOR NIVE & JOOL

A poem is made of words. A very simple poem may be a very few, simple words.

 BUGS

I am very fond of bugs.
I kiss them
And I give them hugs.

TAKE A WORD LIKE CAT

Take a word like cat
And build around it;
A fur room over here
A long meow
Floating from the chimney like a smoke tail.
Draw with words.
Balance them like blocks.
Carve word furniture:
A jar of pussy willows,
Catkins, phlox,
Milk in a dish,
Catnip pillows,
A silver bell,
A plaster bird,
An eaten fish.
When everything is perfect in its place
Step back to view the home
That you have built of words around your word.
It is a poem.

As you read a poem aloud listen to the sounds of the words. They have infinite variety. There are short, brittle sounds, soft rolling sounds, stuttering sounds and the sibilance of many s's, long liquid sounds flowing with o's. In some poems there is not so much sense as sound. Tongue twisters use words in this way. This poem begins like a tongue twister.

THISTLES

Thirty thirsty thistles
Thicketed and green
Growing in a grassy swamp
Purple-topped and lean
Prickly and thistly
Topped by tufts of thorns
Green mean little leaves on them
And tiny purple horns
Briary and brambly
A spiky, spiney bunch of them.
A troop of bright-red birds came by
And had a lovely lunch of them.

LEANDER

Leander, Leander,
I will not meander
Out after a gander with you.
The rills are too rilly,
The hills are too hilly,
The sky is too sparkling blue.
The sun is too low
And the moon is too high,
The dewdrops are dripping,
There's flounder to fry.
There's bacon and cake
And a number of slices
Of Limburger cheese,
And there also are ices.
Meander, Leander,
I say it with candor,
Return here whenever you wish
And we will eat gander
Upon the veranda
Out of a light lavender dish . . .
With fish.

THE PORCUPINE

I watched a weeping porcupine
Come wending through the wildsome wood.
He rested near a mossy patch.
He sniffed and whiffed.
He sadly stood.
With woeful breath
He huffed and puffed,
While I spied smiling there,
And quills and quills
And quills and quills
Shot through the quill-filled air.
He wandered on,
That porcupine,
Loud laughing o'er the hills,
And now 'tis he
Is filled with glee.
'Tis me that's filled with quills.

The words in a poem are like the colors in a painting.
When they are put together with care, they make an
engaging picture.

Imagine that it is a very dark night, just a star or
two, black sky and the moon: round, white. A full moon.
Then the dogs dance out.

 ## FULL OF THE MOON

It's full of the moon
The dogs dance out
Through brush and bush and bramble.
They howl and yowl
And growl and prowl.
They amble, ramble, scramble.
They rush through brush.
They push through bush.
They yip and yap and hurr.
They lark around and bark around
With prickles in their fur.
They two-step in the meadow.
They polka on the lawn.
Tonight's the night
The dogs dance out
And chase their tails till dawn.

This poem seemed to write itself. When I began it, I had one picture in my mind; by the end, I had a totally different one. It was very surprising.

WRITE ABOUT A RADISH

Write about a radish
Too many people write about the moon.

The night is black
The stars are small and high
The clock unwinds its ever-ticking tune
Hills gleam dimly
Distant nighthawks cry.
A radish rises in the waiting sky.

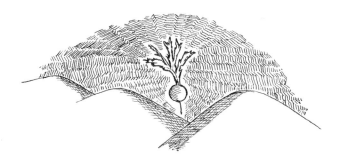

WHERE WOULD YOU BE?

Where would you be on a night like this
With the wind so dark and howling?
Close to the light
Wrapped warm and tight
Or there where the cats are prowling?

Where would you wish you on such a night
When the twisting trees are tossed?
Safe in a chair
In the lamp-lit air
Or out where the moon is lost?

Where would you be when the white waves roar
On the tumbling storm-torn sea?
Tucked inside
Where it's calm and dry
Or searching for stars in the furious sky
Whipped by the whine of the gale's wild cry
Out in the night with me?

That last poem contains a sound like the pounding of wind, waves, rain. That is in the rhythm. Rhythm may be the most important ingredient in a poem. While a poem doesn't need to rhyme—many wonderful poems do not—it must have rhythm. Rhythm gives nonsense verse its bounce. It makes serious lines move with a deliberate beat. Each verse in this silly rhyme has a different, dancy rhythm.

A DANCE

One, two,
One, two,
Hark to the horn
And the tender kazoo.

They're playing our song,
It's a waltz, I believe,
Shall we drift through the draft
With your hand on my sleeve?
Shall we slip on our slippers
And skip side by side
As we airily, merrily, warily glide?

Heel, toe,
Heel, toe,
Curtsy and caper
And over you go.
Toe, heel,
Toe, heel,
The tin trumpets toot
And the violins squeal.
The melody mounts
From a reel to a roar,
We sweep 'cross the carpet
And crash to the floor.

One, two,
One, two,
A man with a mustache
Is wearing my shoe.

SPRING

I'm shouting
I'm singing
I'm swinging through trees
I'm winging sky-high
With the buzzing black bees.
I'm the sun
I'm the moon
I'm the dew on the rose.
I'm a rabbit
Whose habit
Is twitching his nose.
I'm lively
I'm lovely
I'm kicking my heels.
I'm crying "Come dance"
To the freshwater eels.
I'm racing through meadows
Without any coat
I'm a gamboling lamb
I'm a light leaping goat
I'm a bud
I'm a bloom
I'm a dove on the wing.
I'm running on rooftops
And welcoming spring!

SNOW

We'll play in the snow
And stray in the snow
And stay in the snow
In a snow-white park.
We'll clown in the snow
And frown in the snow
Fall down in the snow
Till it's after dark.
We'll cook snow pies
In a big snow pan.
We'll make snow eyes
In a round snow man.
We'll sing snow songs
And chant snow chants
And roll in the snow
In our fat snow pants.
And when it's time to go home to eat
We'll have snow toes
On our frosted feet.

The variety of rhythms in poetry seems endless. Think of the verses that accompany ball playing and jumping rope, the light pattering or heavy drumming of rain on the roof, a disco beat, marching. In some poems and song lyrics, repeating certain lines or words gives them a special rhythm. This poem starts like a march.

LEWIS HAS A TRUMPET

A trumpet
A trumpet
Lewis has a trumpet
A bright one that's yellow
A loud proud horn.
He blows it in the evening
When the moon is newly rising
He blows it when it's raining
In the cold and misty morn
It honks and it whistles
It roars like a lion
It rumbles like a lion
With a wheezy huffing hum
His parents say it's awful
Oh really simply awful
But
Lewis says he loves it
It's such a handsome trumpet
And when he's through with trumpets
He's going to buy a drum.

THE MIDDLE OF THE NIGHT

This is a song to be sung at night
When nothing is left of you and the light
When the cats don't bark
And the mice don't moo
And the nightmares come and nuzzle you
When there's blackness in the cupboards
And the closet and the hall
And a tipping, tapping, rapping
In the middle of the wall
When the lights have one by one gone out
All over everywhere
And a shadow by the curtains
Bumps a shadow by the chair
Then you hide beneath your pillow
With your eyes shut very tight
And you sing
"There's nothing sweeter than
The middle of the night.
I'm extremely fond of shadows
And I really must confess
That cats and bats don't scare me.
Well, they couldn't scare me less
And most of all I like the things
That slide and slip and creep."
It really is surprising
How fast you fall asleep.

*Often the rhythm of a poem is so strong that it alone
holds a poem together. This poem doesn't rhyme at all.
Its strength is in the pattern of the rhythm.*

DAYS THAT THE WIND TAKES OVER

Days that the wind takes over
Blowing through the gardens
Blowing birds out of the street trees
Blowing cats around corners
Blowing my hair out
Blowing my heart apart
Blowing high in my head
Like the sea sound caught in a shell.
One child put her thin arms around the wind
And they went off together.
Later the wind came back
Alone.

Many poems are descriptions of places, moods, things. Describe your cat. A good description doesn't tell you everything about that cat, but it uses a few special details arranged with care. It is these details and their special arrangement that make a particular picture.

THIS CAT

This cat
Walks into the room and across the floor,
Under a chair, around the bed,
Behind the table and out the door.
I'm sitting on the chair
And I don't see where he is.
I don't see one hair of his.
I just hear the floorboards scarcely squeak.
This cat comes and goes
On invisible toes.
The sneak.

Or the description may be silly.

ME

"My nose is blue,
My teeth are green,
My face is like a soup tureen.
I look just like a lima bean.
I'm very, very lovely.
My feet are far too short
And long.
My hands are left and right
And wrong.
My voice is like the hippo's song.
I'm very, very,
Very, very,
Very, very
Lovely?"

THE PORTLY OBJECT

There was a man who was so fat
He wore a bathtub for a hat.
He wore a basin for a shoe,
And if you do not think this true
You've but to look across the square,
You see those mountains standing there
Between the sky-blue sky and lawn?
Well, one has got a bathtub on.

Another kind of description is a list of many details. The list is held together with word sounds and rhythm.

THE MEAL

Timothy Tompkins had turnips and tea.
The turnips were tiny.
He ate at least three.
And then, for dessert,
He had onions and ice.
He liked that so much
That he ordered it twice.
He had two cups of ketchup,
A prune, and a pickle.
"Delicious," said Timothy.
"Well worth a nickel."
He folded his napkin
And hastened to add,
"It's one of the loveliest breakfasts I've had."

WILLIAM'S TOYS

William has a dump truck
And piles of blocks.
William has some stamps
And coins
And thirty-seven rocks,
A racing car, a dancing bear,
A lion that can roar.
William has a helmet
That his Uncle Arthur wore.
He has pencils. He has soldiers.
He has crayons. He has bats
And mitts and balls,
A tricycle and seven cowboy hats,
Guns that squirt,
A turtle and a baby guinea pig,
A set of trains, some cars and cranes
And shovels, small and big,
Paints in pints, and brushes,
A telescope, a clock

That comes apart, a tugboat
And a set to make a dock
With a lighthouse and a liner,
Some glasses without glass,
An arrowhead that William found
And William took to class,
Marbles, checkers, packs of cards
And books and books and books,
Shells from summer beaches
And stones from summer brooks,
Leaves, now dry, a butterfly
Pinned neatly to a board,
A motorboat that's broken,
A silver rubber sword,
An ambulance that winds and winds
To make the siren's noise.
William says he's bored because
He needs some other toys.

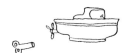

CATHERINE

Catherine said, "I think I'll bake
A most delicious chocolate cake."
She took some mud and mixed it up
While adding water from a cup
And then some weeds and nuts and bark
And special gravel from the park
A thistle and a dash of sand.
She beat out all the lumps by hand.
And on the top she wrote "To You"
The way she says the bakers do
And then she signed it "Fondly, C."
And gave the whole of it to me.
I thanked her but I wouldn't dream
Of eating cake without ice cream.

All poetry should be read aloud sometimes. Read this aloud as fast as you can.

JOE'S SNOW CLOTHES

For wandering walks
In the sparkling snow
No one is muffled
More warmly than Joe.
No one is mittened more,
Coated or hatted,
Booted or sweatered,
Both knitted and tatted,
Buttoned and zippered,
Tied, tucked and belted,
Padded and wadded
And quilted and felted,
Hooked in and hooded,
Tweeded and twilled.
Nothing of Joe's
From his top to his toes
But the tip of his nose
Could be touched
By the snows
Or the wind as it blows,
And grow rather rosy,
The way a nose grows
If it's frozen
Or possibly chilled.

In order to describe something you have to look at it closely, see it with a clear eye and remember it. Writing and remembering are like Siamese twins; they are so close to each other and so hard to separate. They need each other. Parts of the past are always showing up in the words you write.

SPRING AGAIN

Spring again
Spring again
Spring again
Isn't it?
Buds on the branches
A breeze in the blue
And me without mittens
My sweater unbuttoned
A spring full of things
All before me to do.

THE SNAKE

A snake slipped through the thin green grass
A silver snake
I watched it pass
It moved like a ribbon
Silent as snow.
I think it smiled
As it passed my toe.

THE TREE AND ME

There's a tree by the meadow
By the sand by the sea
On a hillock near a valley
That belongs to me
With small spring leaves
Like small green dimes
That cast their shadows on the grass
A thousand separate times
With round brown branches
Like outstretched sleeves
And the twigs come out as fingers
And the fingers hold the leaves
With blossoms here and there
And always pink and soft and stout
And when the blossoms disappear
The apples hurry out
And
In the middle of the blossoms
In the center of the tree
With a hat and coat of leaves on
Sits smiling me.

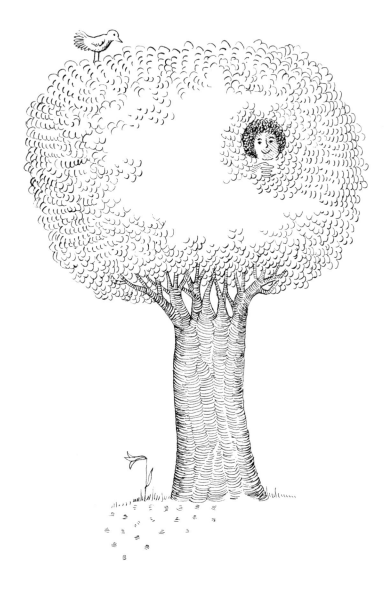

TIPTOE

Yesterday I skipped all day,
The day before I ran,
Today I'm going to tiptoe
Everywhere I can.
I'll tiptoe down the stairway.
I'll tiptoe through the door.
I'll tiptoe to the living room
And give an awful roar
And my father, who is reading,
Will jump up from his chair
And mumble something silly like
"I didn't see you there."
I'll tiptoe to my mother
And give a little cough
And when she spins to see me
Why, I'll softly tiptoe off.
I'll tiptoe through the meadows,
Over hills and yellow sands
And when my toes get tired
Then I'll tiptoe on my hands.

WHEN I WENT OUT

When I went out to see the sun
There wasn't sun or anyone
But there was only sand and sea
And lots of rain that fell on me
And where the rain and river met
The water got completely wet.

SITTING IN THE SAND

Sitting in the sand and the sea comes up
So you put your hands together
And you use them like a cup
And you dip them in the water
With a scooping kind of motion
And before the sea goes out again
You have a sip of ocean.

BEACHES

There are reaches of beaches
With nothing but sand
Where you go with a shovel
A pail and a friend
And you dig there together
Well into the winter
The summer
The autumn
The former
The latter.
Years pass and you leave
Walking off hand in hand.
It doesn't much matter
How long you both dig there,
The sand will not end.

COUNTING

To count myself
Is quickly done.
There's never more of me
Than one.

Counting bears
Is fun by ones
But funnier in pairs.

Counting the birds
On the branches of trees
Is hard on the neck
But it's easy on the knees.

It's even harder
Counting leaves
Than counting tiny birds.
They shift their shadows
With the breeze
Among the branches
Of the trees
More numerous
Than whispered words.

Counting fingers
And counting toes is
A harder kind of counting
Than counting noses.

Counting rabbits running
Rabbit races on the lawn
Must be done while one is sunning
And before a rabbit's gone.

Counting the stars
As they glitter bright white
Is lovely indeed
And a marvelous sight
When the air is as fresh
As the first night in fall.
But I always have a feeling
That comes very softly stealing
When my head with stars is reeling
That I didn't count them all.

FALL

When I go walking in the fall
I stop to watch the deer.
They open up their lovely eyes
And blink
And disappear.
The rabbits hop from here
To there
And in
And out
And under
While deep within the forest heart
The black bears roar like thunder.
The chipmunks gather butternuts
And hide them in a tree
Where clever squirrels
Discover them
And laugh with squirrelish glee.
My hat is green
My jacket blue
With patches on the sleeves
And as I walk
I crunch through piles
Of red and yellow leaves.

AROUND AND AROUND

The flower's on the bird
Which is underneath the bee
And the bird is on the kitten
On the cat on me.
I'm on a chair
On some grass
On a lawn
And the lawn is on a meadow
And the world is what it's on.
And all of us together
When the day is nearly done
Like to sit and watch the weather
As we spin around the sun.

This poem describes two things, a memory and a feeling.

IT IS GREY OUT

It is grey out.
It is grey in.
In me
It is as grey as the day is grey.
The trees look sad
And I,
Not knowing why I do,
Cry.

Many memories are memories of feelings. The first two poems in this group are about the same time of day, but each describes a very different feeling.

VERY EARLY

When I wake in the early mist
The sun has hardly shown
And everything is still asleep
And I'm awake alone.
The stars are faint and flickering.
The sun is new and shy.
And all the world sleeps quietly,
Except the sun and I.
And then beginning noises start,
The whrrrs and huffs and hums,
The birds peep out to find a worm,
The mice squeak out for crumbs,
The calf moos out to find the cow,
And taste the morning air
And everything is wide awake
And running everywhere.
The dew has dried,
The fields are warm,
The day is loud and bright,
And I'm the one who woke the sun
And kissed the stars good night.

 **I WOKE UP THIS MORNING**

I woke up this morning
At quarter past seven.
I kicked up the covers
And stuck out my toe.

And ever since then
(That's a quarter past seven)
They haven't said anything
Other than "no."

They haven't said anything
Other than "Please, dear,
Don't do what you're doing,"
Or "Lower your voice."

Whatever I've done
And however I've chosen,
I've done the wrong thing
And I've made the wrong choice.

I didn't wash well
And I didn't say thank you.
I didn't shake hands
And I didn't say please.

I didn't say sorry

When passing the candy

I banged the box into

Miss Witelson's knees.

I didn't say sorry.

I didn't stand straighter.

I didn't speak louder

When asked what I'd said.

Well, I said
That tomorrow
At quarter past seven
They can
Come in and get me.
I'm Staying In Bed.

THE QUESTION

People always say to me
"What do you think you'd like to be
When you grow up?"
And I say "Why,
I think I'd like to be the sky
Or be a plane or train or mouse
Or maybe be a haunted house
Or something furry, rough and wild . . .
Or maybe I will stay a child."

This is a conversation between a mother and her child.
I have been the mother in conversations like this. Years
ago I was the child.

WHERE HAVE YOU BEEN DEAR?

Where
Have you been dear?
What
Have you seen dear?
What
Did you do there?
Who
Went with you there?
Tell me
What's new dear?
What's
New with you dear?
Where
Will you go next?
What
Will you do?

"I do this and I do that.
I go here and I go there.
At times I like to be alone.
There are some thoughts that are my own
I do not wish to share."

A poem often tells a story. Sometimes very short, sometimes long.

A BUG SAT IN A SILVER FLOWER

A bug sat in a silver flower
Thinking silver thoughts.
A bigger bug out for a walk
Climbed up that silver flower stalk
And snapped the small bug down his jaws
Without a pause
Without a care
For all the bug's small silver thoughts.
It isn't right
It isn't fair
That big bug ate that little bug
Because that little bug was there.

He also ate his underwear.

HUGHBERT AND THE GLUE

Hughbert had a jar of glue.
From Hugh the glue could not be parted,
At least could not be parted far,
For Hugh was glued to Hughbert's jar.
But that is where it all had started.
The glue upon the shoe of Hugh
Attached him to the floor.
The glue on Hughbert's gluey hand
Was fastened to the door,
While two of Hughbert's relatives
Were glued against each other.
His mother, I believe, was one.
The other was his brother.
The dog and cat stood quite nearby.
They could not move from there.
The bird was glued securely
Into Hughbert's mother's hair.

Hughbert's father hurried home
And loudly said to Hugh:
"From now on I would rather
That you did not play with glue."

 I HAVE A LION

I had a cat,
Grey
Soft
Fat
Given to grrrring
Quite softly
And prrrrring.
Slipped off one morning
Near the green glen.
That was my cat
Who was not seen again.

I had a dog,
Noisy and yellow
Very cold nose
Wonderful fellow.
Trotted one evening
Out after a pack
Of dog-footed friends
And never came back.

I had a bird,
Bright blue in a cage
Sang without cease
On his miniature stage.
Sat on my shoulder
Looked in my eye
Sailed out the window
And into the sky.

I have a lion,
Furry and kind
Sits on a shelf
Near the autos that wind.
Eyes wild and golden
Tail like a tuft
He never will slip out and leave me.
He's stuffed.

THE BEAR WITH GOLDEN HAIR

Long ago
There was a bear
With ice-blue eyes
And golden hair
And pale-pink paws,
A bright black nose,
And a shiny, silken ribbon
More red than rose.

But though he was a perfect bear,
He had one secret, deep despair:
He did not have a thing to wear
Except a lot of golden hair.
"I wish,"
He'd sigh,
"I had a pair
Of socks or shoes
In reds or blues.
Some pale-plaid pants
I'd also choose."
For hours he would sit and muse
On splendid clothes
That he would wear
Were he not such a fair-haired bear.

One Wednesday
Also long ago,
This gold-haired bear
Went to and fro
To see the spring
And sniff the bud,
When Amelia Ellen Whitely,
Who was holding him quite tightly,
Tripped a little more than slightly
And he fell into the mud.

Amelia Ellen had to stare.
There lay her once-so-golden bear
Now muddied up from here to there.

Now muddied down from there to here,
From toe to toe
To ear to ear
To heel to heel
To knee to nose;
His ribbon hanging limply down,
A wet and brackish
Blackish brown,
A lot more mud than rose.

She took him home
And ran the tub
And started in to soap and scrub,
To comb and brush,
To rinse and rub.
From dusk she worked
Into the dawn,
And as the sunlight lit the lawn
No mud was there upon her bear.
But, oh,
Amelia had to stare,
His hair was also gone.

Then, her needle threaded tightly,
Amelia Ellen Whitely
Stitched with energy and care
Daily, noon, and nightly.
She made bear pairs
Of socks and shoes
In rosey reds and azure blues,
Jackets,
Gloves,
And pale-plaid pants
At which each passerby would glance,
Exclaiming with approving "oh's."
"I say, my dear,
Do give a stare
At yonder very-well-dressed bear.
If I but had such splendid clothes."

Long ago
There was a bear
Without a single golden hair.
He also did not have a care.
Oh, happy hair-free carefree bear.

When you draw, you may draw something real or make up a whole landscape. Or perhaps your drawing will combine what you see with what you imagine. When you write you have the same choices. You may write about something that really happened, or something that could never have happened. Reality can lead you to imagining, and the imagination has no boundaries. Anything can happen in the world that is inside your head.

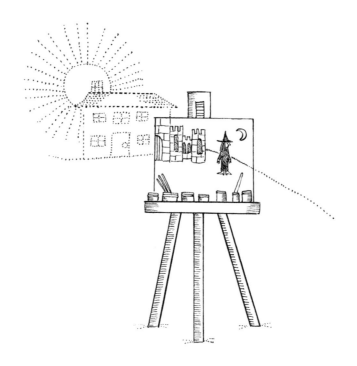

THE GOLD-TINTED DRAGON

What's the good of a wagon
Without any dragon
To pull you for mile after mile?
An elegant lean one
A gold-tinted green one
Wearing a dragonly smile.
You'll sweep down the valleys
You'll sail up the hills
Your dragon will shine in the sun
And as you rush by
The people will cry
"I wish that my wagon had one!"

KNITTED THINGS

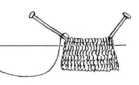

There was a witch who knitted things:
Elephants and playground swings.
She knitted rain,
She knitted night,
But nothing really came out right.
The elephants had just one tusk
And night looked more
Like dawn or dusk.
The rain was snow
And when she tried
To knit an egg
It came out fried.
She knitted birds
With buttonholes
And twenty rubber butter rolls.
She knitted blue angora trees.
She purl stitched countless purple fleas.
She knitted a palace in need of a darn.
She knitted a battle and ran out of yarn.
She drew out a strand
Of her gleaming, green hair
And knitted a lawn
Till she just wasn't there.

THE WITCHES' RIDE

Over the hills
Where the edge of the light
Deepens and darkens
To ebony night,
Narrow hats high
Above yellow bead eyes,
The tatter-haired witches
Ride through the skies.
Over the seas
Where the flat fishes sleep
Wrapped in the slap of the slippery deep,
Over the peaks
Where the black trees are bare,
Where boney birds quiver
They glide through the air.
Silently humming
A horrible tune,
They sweep through the stillness
To sit on the moon.

Imagine that you are not yourself at all but someone or something else. What would you choose?

SQUARE AS A HOUSE

What would you choose
If you were free
To be anything fat
That you wanted to be?
Anything thin or long or tall,
Anything red, blue, black, at all;
A bird on the wing
Or a fish on the fin?
If you're ready to choose
It is time to begin.

If you could be square
Would you be a box
Containing a cake
Or a house
Or blocks
With painted letters
From A to Z?
Who would you
Which would you
What would you be?

If you could be soft
Would you be the snow
Or twenty-five pillows
Or breezes that blow
The blossoms that fall from
The sassafras tree?
Who would you
Which would you
What would you be?

If you could be loud
Would you be the sound
Of thunder at night
Or the howl of a hound
As he bays at the moon
Or the pound of the sea?
Who would you
Which would you
What would you be?

⟹

If you could be small
Would you be a mouse
Or a mouse's child
Or a mouse's house
Or a mouse's house's
Front door key?
Who would you
Which would you
What would you be?

If you could be dark
Would you be the night
Or a house on a hill
Where there wasn't a light
Or a witch watcher
Watching a witch with glee?
Who would you
Which would you
What would you be?

The following five poems do not have titles. As you read each poem you will figure out what it is describing. Each one tells how it would feel to be something other than yourself.

If you stood with your feet in the earth
Up to your ankles in grass
And your arms had leaves running over them
And every once in a while one of your leafy fingers
Was nudged by a bird flying past,
If the skin that covers you from top to tip
Wasn't skin at all, but bark
And you never moved your feet from their place
In the earth
But stood rooted in that one spot come
Rain
Wind
Snow
Sleet
Thaw
Spring
Summer
Winter
Fall
Blight
Bug
Day
Dark
Then you would be me:
A tree.

I liked growing.
That was nice.
The leaves were soft
The sun was hot.
I was warm and red and round
Then someone dropped me in a pot.
Being a strawberry isn't all pleasing.
This morning they put me in ice cream.
I'm freezing.

Let me tell you all about me.
Children love me.
You're a child.
All my heads are green and handsome.
All my eyes are red and wild.
All my toes have claws upon them.
All the claws have hooks.
I blow smoke through all my noses.
It is hotter than it looks.
All my tails have points upon them.
All my teeth are sharp and blue.
I won't bite you very badly.
I am fond of you.
All my scales are shaped like arrows.
They will hurt you if you touch.
So, although I know you'll love me,
Do not pet me very much.

One thing you can say about roaring.
It is not boring.
And if rushing around the jungle being king
Is your kind of thing
You might find the life of a lion
Worth tryin'.

If you,
Like me,
Were made of fur
And sun warmed you,
Like me,
You'd purr.

IF I WERE A . . .

If I were a bird,
I would chirp like a bird
With a high little cry.
I would not say a word.
I would sit in my nest
With my head on my chest,
Being a bird.

If I were a fish,
I would swim like a fish
Silently finning
With nary a swish,
Just finning through seaweed
To search for a free weed,
Being a fish.

If I were a larkspur,
I'd stand in the sun,
Growing up slowly
Until I was done.
I'd rest in the breeze
With some leaves on my knees,
Being a larkspur.

If I were a sandwich,
I'd sit on a plate
And think of my middle
Until someone ate
Me.
End of the sandwich.

What would it be like to be a child who could speak only in rhyme?

ALEXANDER SOAMES: HIS POEMS

Once upon
Upon a time
There was a child
Who spoke in rhyme.
Three tall physicians and a nurse
Have testified
That it was verse.
His hair was brown.
His height was short.
His pants were grey,
The shorter sort.
His name was Alexander Soames
And when he spoke
He spoke in poems.

The first time Alex saw a cat
He did not run,
He simply sat
And said,
"It's flat
That that's
A cat."

And when he saw a dog he said,
Scratching his small poetic head,
"The walk of a dog
Is more of a jog
And less of a dance
Than the amble of ants."

Alexander had a mother.
"Dear," she said a thousand times,
"Dear," she said to Alexander,
"Must you always speak in rhymes?
Wear your rubbers,
Wipe your nose,
Why not try
To speak in prose?"

"I prefer," said Alex Soames,
"To speak the speech I speak
In poems."

Alexander first walked this way.
Alexander then walked that.
"Rhyming suits me," Alex murmured,
"I suit rhyming," and he sat,
Sat and pondered,
Sat and sat.
"I will try once more," said Alex,
"I'll attempt it though I tend
To have doubts about the outcome.
Here's a simple phrase:
            The End."

*The following is an example of Alexander Soames'
poems:*

RULES

Do not jump on ancient uncles.

*

Do not yell at average mice.

*

Do not wear a broom to breakfast.

*

Do not ask a snake's advice.

*

Do not bathe in chocolate pudding.

*

Do not talk to bearded bears.

*

Do not smoke cigars on sofas.

*

Do not dance on velvet chairs.

*

Do not take a whale to visit
Russell's mother's cousin's yacht.

*

And whatever else you do do
It is better you
Do not.

*Dreams are the imaginings of sleep. This verse is almost
a dream. It began to go through my head late one night
as I was falling asleep.*

MOON

Moon
Have you met my mother?
Asleep in a chair there
Falling down hair.

Moon in the sky
Moon in the water
Have you met one another?
Moon face to moon face
Deep in that dark place
Suddenly bright.

Moon
Have you met my friend the night?

DIFFERENT DREAMS

When dusk is done
And the grey has gone
And the stars blow out
That once were on,
Then the pale moon casts
Its frozen gleams
And the hollow of night
Fills up with dreams:
Cats of mice
Elves of trolls
Cooks of silver spoons and bowls.
Poets dream of rhymes and Rome.
Sailors dream of ships and home.
Princes dream of foreign lands
To conquer
And of ladies' hands.
Dogs dream dreams
Of hounds to hares.
The red fox dreams
Of grass-green lairs.
While deep in your sleep,
With your dark eyes shut tight,
You dream of the day
That will follow the night.

If there were a recipe for a poem, these would be the ingredients: word sounds, rhythm, description, feeling, memory, rhyme and imagination. They can be put together a thousand different ways, a thousand, thousand . . . more. If you and I were to go at the same time to the same party for the same person, our descriptions would be different. As different as we are from each other. It is those differences that make our poems interesting.

THE ROSE ON MY CAKE

I went to a party,
A party for Pearly,
With presents and ice cream,
With favors and games.
I stayed very late
And I got there quite early.
I met all the guests
And I know all their names.
We sang and we jumped.
We jumped and we jostled.
We jostled and rustled
At musical chairs.
We ate up the cake
And we folded the candy in baskets
In napkins
We folded in squares.

We blew up balloons
And we danced without shoes.
We danced on the floor
And the rug and the bed.
We tripped and we trotted
In trios and twos.
And I neatly balanced myself
On my head.
Pearly just smiled
As she blew out the candles.
I gave the rose from my cake
To a friend,
Millicent Moss,
In her black patent sandals.
The trouble with parties is
All of them end.

Even the ways we say good-bye are different. They may be as distinctive as our handwriting or the sounds of our voices.

THOUGHTS THAT WERE PUT INTO WORDS

Thoughts that were put into words
Have been said.
The words were then spoken
And written
And read.
Take a look and go on
We are practically done.

The leftover afternoon light
Slips away
On a wind like a sigh.
Watch the day curtains close,
Hear the wind going grey
At the edge of the edge
You and I
Turn the page
Read its message
"The End."

Does the end mean good-bye?

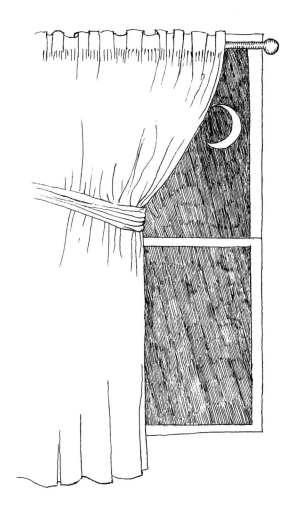

Index